MW01534895

BOUNDARIES AT WORK

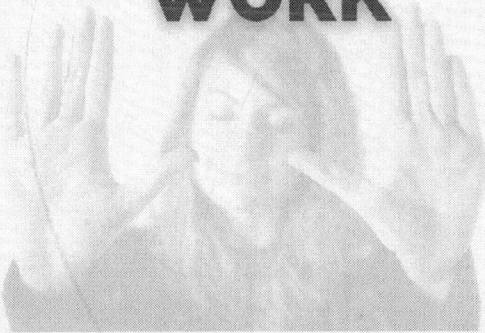

A Guide to Establishing
Boundaries, Protecting Your
Time, Energy, Sanity, And
Boosting Productivity at Work

HEIDI W. SORENSEN

Copyright ©2023 by Heidi W. Sorensen. All rights reserved.

No part of this publication may be reproduced, stored in a retrieval system, or transmitted in any form or by any means, electronic, mechanical, photocopying, recording, scanning, or otherwise, without the publisher's prior written permission.

This book is sold subject to the condition that it shall not, by way of trade or otherwise, be lent, resold, hired out, or otherwise circulated without the publisher's prior consent in any form of binding or cover other than that in which it is published and without a similar condition including this condition being imposed on the subsequent purchaser.

TABLE OF CONTENTS

INTRODUCTION

Are you feeling overwhelmed, anxious, or overworked at work? Do you wish for clearer boundaries to safeguard your time, energy, and sanity? This is a book for you.

In today's fast-paced, ever-changing workplace, setting boundaries is more vital than ever. Establishing good limits can make all the difference between stress and happiness.

Let me give you a quick story to introduce this book. A few years ago, I had a friend who worked as a project manager for a prominent company.

She was constantly stressed and overworked despite her dedication to her profession and enjoyment of working with her colleagues. She would leave the office late, carry her work home, and check her email all night. She believed she had insufficient time for her family and friends.

She recognized one day that action was required. She established limits for herself. This includes leaving work at a decent hour, withdrawing from the office after hours, and putting her own life first. She discovered that she was happier, less anxious, and more productive at work.

Consider this: At work, you stare blankly at the computer monitor. Feeling weary and overloaded. You are inundated with work and requests from your employer and coworkers.

Your work is frequently interrupted by phone calls and meetings, leaving you with little time to complete your tasks. You feel exhausted and anxious, wondering whether this will be your professional life forever.

Does this sound familiar?

Due to competing demands, short deadlines, and constant performance pressure, modern workplaces can be challenging to navigate. It is easy to lose sight of your needs and priorities in the chaos. It does not have to be this way.

This book will show you how to establish healthy workplace boundaries to safeguard your energy, productivity, time, and mental health. This book will aid you in taking charge of your professional life and establishing clear limits.

Additionally, it will assist you in achieving equilibrium in your work relationships. Establishing appropriate boundaries will make you more productive, experience less stress, and achieve your goals.

Let's get started if you are prepared to take charge of your work life, and attain greater balance, productivity, well-being, and control.

CHAPTER 1

The Power of Work Boundaries

Although work-life balance is not a popular topic, it is important to pay attention. An imbalance in work life can severely affect employees' personal and professional lives.

This can cause increased stress, anxiety, depression, and other negative effects. It can cause problems in family relationships and work performance (such as decreased output or lack of creativity) and burnout. What can you do to avoid these negative consequences?

It is easier than you think. You can set clear boundaries between work and your personal life.

What do Work Boundaries Look like?

The "work boundary" refers to any action you take to separate your work day from other days. It can be anything like a morning cup or evening glass of wine. It could also be an action taken during work hours.

For example, you could visit a nearby coffee shop to meet your morning meeting.

Many people have difficulty defining boundaries between work and personal lives. It is a matter of play and recreation. Most people feel that they are allowed to have some control over actual play, such as what they do for leisure or entertainment.

What about work? Why are we so compelled to play in an office environment, even though it's a job we do for a living? We are living under an illusion.

Our workspace is not an issue. Work happens in a separate bubble from our lives at home and work. The truth is that every job you do has a greater impact on your life than you may think.

People choose to live an intentional lifestyle, which means they set priorities and manage their time accordingly (e.g., spending quality time with family).

We are all hurting in our work worlds. Although we can look at all the statistics to see that work stress is rising, we don't need to. We can feel it in our bodies. There's tension, physical pain, insomnia, and a bit of unresolved friction in our families. Maybe we want more time together.

We always seem to need more this is also evident in our communities.

- Our political systems could be better.
- Our educational systems are in dire need of support. Even our local gatherings bring us together but leave us bitterly divided.
- This space is for 10.

I learned to work hard to pursue my dreams and make them come true. My mother, a powerful worker, is 50 per cent equal to my father. There were also challenges.

My parents worked crazy hours, and 60 to 65 was the norm. 70 to 80 were expected, and family movie night consisted of us all going to the local video shop. We'd buy one or two VHS's then put that in the video.

We'd enjoy pizza together, but my parents would disappear into the background. My mother was surrounded by paperwork by her father. He was going through his weekly to-do list and taping off the rest of the actions. I was excited to join that workforce.

It was hard work, but it wasn't easy. In my 20s, i struggled with chronic back pain. I remember leaning over the edge and trying to lift my leg above my left ankle.

Physical pain. That moment was when i realized that something had to change in my approach to work. I tried a lot of physical therapy and yoga to manage my back pain. This eventually led me to mindfulness and meditation.

It's only one component of stress management. But, it is just one component of a larger conversation about work boundaries. At the end of the week, stress management will only support me if my work is relaxed.

Let's review some statistics from the International Labor Organization. They define excessively long work hours as more than 48 hours per week. These work hours can lead to poor outcomes in terms of both health and work performance.

The average salaried full-time employee in the United States works 49 hours per week. I say this because it is important to understand our current situation.

We all do the same thing and wonder if there is a better way. And we wouldn't dare to challenge that system for fear of the consequences. But here's the deal: we won't solve the biggest problems in our organization or the biggest challenges facing the world. We will be exhausted, depleted, and drained. This is why I share my self-care model.

Boundaries are another way I like to think about it. Energy plus choice equals energy. It can be used wherever you are.

Number two, it's easy, and it grows through the application. I have learned that the best tools are simple but offer huge leverage on the back end.

Reason number three continually strengthens the individual and the self at all stages of the equation. If there's one thing we've learned from this pandemic, it's that resilient organization are built by resilient individuals.

Let's look at self-care. I remember when i first got into self-care. I would wait until the end of my days five, six, seven, or eight to finally take that deep breath. Friday night was always a great night. I'd go out with friends to have a drink and finally relax.

You have to be persistent to achieve that moment.

You can then identify the tools, practices, and support strategies you have for yourself in each of these locations. If you take it one step further, you can also identify how often you do it. This is because it is about my ability to connect with my environment and my inner self. It is about my authentic yes and no and how that is communicated externally. Boundaries are hard. I have had to confront fears that I didn't know existed.

It's made me look at my beliefs and mindsets that have kept me stuck for years. We would be remiss if it didn't.

CHAPTER 2

Boundaries With Boss

It can be very frustrating to feel like your boss constantly checks on you or tells you what to do. Having a professional relationship with them can be hard when they are so insistent and pushy.

Here are some tips to help you develop a better relationship.

It is important first to ask why your boss seems so overbearing. You might feel overwhelmed by their busy schedule and are trying to manage everyone. Sometimes they need to learn how to get results for everyone else in the office.

Instead of taking their behavior personally, ask them if anything is wrong with the situation or if there are any ways you could improve it. They might not realize they are being pushy. So, give them a chance.

This chapter will cover how to manage your boss by setting healthy boundaries.

If they're inexperienced or have other issues that make them difficult to deal with in management literature, the way you manage your boss's behavior is called managing up. Tip number one:

Identify your limits and permit yourself to do so.

Create a list that lists all the times you feel you've been pushed past your limits.

Write down the reasons you feel this way.

Be specific.

You should also tell yourself it's not a personal attack. And so, you're not blaming them; it's really on you that you haven't campaigned for this previously, so you also have to distinguish whether this is self-care or selfishness.

So, by going through this initial stage, you identify your boundaries and feelings and see that you're not honoring your limits, which is why you're harboring resentment inside.

So that's an important step. The second tip is actually to meet set expectations. This may appear stupid, but you must sit down and set the expectations through open communication, so it is part of your job and your boss's duty to understand and respect your boundaries.

Two sorts of communication are crucial to creating boundaries.

The first type involves having an expected dialogue

To establish stronger boundaries, you must first understand what your supervisor believes you can and should do.

Several guiding questions can help with this, such as who I report to, who provides feedback, who decides what I should be working on, and what are the few things you need me to accomplish in the short or medium term.

What does success look like, when do you expect this to be completed, and how will it be measured?

When I'm there, you can negotiate unrealistic timelines to make them more feasible, and that's a critical step in developing that knowledge of expectations so that you understand where they're coming from and their point of view.

The style talk is the second type of conversation, and it is about allowing you to re-examine the style with which you and your supervisor engage.

Guiding questions for that would be what kinds of decisions your boss wants to be involved in and where you can decide on your own if your style is deferred, and what are the implications for how you should interact working this all would give you a much deeper understanding of where the boundaries are.

This part is super important, so I define time to sit down with your boss and work out the expectations and style of you two working together.

You'll also be able to set boundaries during non-work hours and learn about their expectations, but it will also allow you to explain your boundaries, which you should have sorted out in the previous phase.

Remember that a healthy boundary allows you to exercise control over what you allow while preventing you from becoming unduly defensive or resistant to change.

Things you can address include the expected email or messaging turnaround times during non-work hours if any, and What about the weekends?

How about calls to work and weekly check-ins to avoid spontaneous drop-ins to each other that can be distracting? You can only debate whether you should leave your work laptop at work, stop working completely during vacation days, or take time to be offline.

Also, if a social network friend gets engaged, closing your office door or using headphones to signal do not disturb is preferable to embracing.

Things like app to work socializing are all things you can cover well the third thing you can do is create a boundary statement and this one you need to decide for yourself.

How far you want to take it because your boss is different from everyone else's bosses right it really depends and you may just want to write it down for yourself or you may want to involve your boss and co-creating it if your boss is really cool that right it totally depends on your boss right it totally depends on your boss right it totally depends on your boss.

It will help you be more motivated and productive at work if you and your boss agree on the best way to get things done at work and at home if necessary, and you want to write it down for reference or examples of what can go in a boundary statement can include.

If my boss emails me at 8 p.m., I answer it by 12 p.m. the next day, or if my boss texts me during dinner, I do not respond until after dinner, or Remember to ask them to acknowledge rather than approve it because for after-work stuff, you really don't need their approval so you don't even open that door right just ask them to acknowledge it so whatever your boss says and you have to deal with this with some time.

If your boss pushes back against you having no boundaries statement or having like you know a formal description off your boundaries you need to think about this sign carefully what does this say about your boss Jot down notes after the meeting.

When it's fresh in your mind so that you can refer to them in the future whether it's for your own personal use or for a co-use or, as I said before, it depends on the situation so keep it for your reference or pin it somewhere at home so that you know what the protocol is when the time comes and if your boss texts you during dinner.

Be prepared to face opposition as well. If that's the case, it's probably time to reconsider the boundaries. If there is a bilateral boundary agreement, which is an agreement that both parties agree on, use it; if not, go off on the one that you wrote immediately after the meeting right and use that as a point of reference like hey boss.

I wrote this down immediately after I met with you previously, which makes me uncomfortable we talked about this right. Hence, you must enforce that you have let them know there may be emergent situations. Whether you and your boss draft this boundary statement together or separately, you have something to go off of if necessary.

It's going to be an ongoing process that will take time for you and your boss to figure out, and you guys might change as well.

You might become more comfortable with your boss, or your boundaries may vary, so it's a point of reference, but it's not set in stone. Fifth, know your rights.

This last tip is entirely up to you if you feel the need to go there, but many people need to be fully aware of the extent of their rights at work.

In most developed countries, there are protections in place that are generally deemed off-limits at work. For example, in Ontario, where I live, the Employment Standards Act states that the Ontario Human Rights Code protects people from employment discrimination based on race and ethnicity.

So, these are all things that are your rights, which you should not put in your boundary statement because they're super sensitive topics. Still, they're unspoken but legally binding employment laws, so if you feel that any of these unspoken but legally binding employment boundaries were crossed, it makes you uncomfortable.

CHAPTER 3

Coworkers Are Not Your Friends

It can be hard to imagine colleagues walking the same streets and meeting you at a similar water cooler. Yet, despite working together day in and day out, we still have difficulty working with them.

This disconnect is caused by: This is because coworkers often need to be better informed to establish any relationship.

This can result in a hostile work environment, where everyone always plays a team tennis game rather than getting anything done.

Because they don't get along and respect each other, they can't trust one another deeply. They also don't share confidential information necessary for collaboration (such as their best ideas).

However, the problem continues. Working relationships that are often superficial only last for a bit longer than the surface. People are so busy trying to finish their projects that they don't have enough time to connect meaningfully.

Here is where you start seeing the disconnect between work and personal life. We should be more focused on what we have to do instead of enjoying each other and building relationships that last a lifetime.

It is often those who work together that we spend the most time during the day. Workers spend more time working with their coworkers than with their immediate family and friends.

It's easy for coworkers to get too close. What is the difference between work friends and real friends? Keep in mind that colleagues at work are not your friends. Here are some of the dangers associated with being friends at work.

There are reasons why work colleagues are not your friends

1. Promotion over Coworker

It can be very frustrating to get promoted ahead of your colleague. You might have both wanted the promotion, but your boss decided to give it to you. Your coworker might dislike you. They may try to undermine you out of jealousy or defy you.

Because they likely see you as one, your pals won't take you seriously when you suddenly become a group leader.

Because you want your friends to stay away, giving the appropriate punishments may take a lot of work. It is possible to avoid all tension by telling them, "I'm here for work, not to make friends."

2. Protection for colleagues

A coworker might ask you to take care of them if they need to be more active. Your manager may request that you lie to them when you inquire about them.

If you do not, your coworker and you can get into a heated argument. The office could become a stressful environment you only look forward to sometimes.

However, if you cover for them, your supervisor may find out. You should look at ways to get away from coworkers before you experience severe professional consequences that could cause you to lose your job.

3. Incapability to issue a Warning

Let's say your employer wants to terminate one of your coworkers. You must prepare them for the worst by giving them prior notice so they can look for other work.

They are your friend. They will be furious if you tell them you weren't aware of their existence and do not inform you.

But your boss won't allow you to tell them. You are forced to keep your silence even though it may bring you down.

4. Do not divulge too many details that may endanger your career

You can consider your colleague's friends and what might stop you from sharing your personal details. You could tell your colleagues that you missed a meeting due to having a wild night out with close friends or that you woke up with a bad hangover.

Because you have just shared your friend's data, you may believe your data is secure. The speed at which rumors spread is something you need to remember.

A coworker could have trusted another coworker with this information. The information may be passed on to your employer. Your employer will then fire you because they cannot handle an employee who isn't committed.

Always pay attention to your coworkers; they will work for the money and choose stability over you. Fake friends at the office are all too common. You have to be yourself and keep your professional ambitions and personal life separate from them.

5. Love Drama

Coworkers are worse than friends, so avoiding dating them is better. A coworker can cause more Drama at work than just talking to them. Unfortunately, many of these partnerships fail.

We all know that half of all marriages end up in divorce. This is false, though, since divorce rates have fallen to around 25% for the average married couple.

Now, think about the high divorce rate of married people. What happens to a new relationship? Your chances of ending a relationship with someone you work with increase when they are in the same office. This is because you spend more time with them than on their virtues.

Your relationship could end and make it difficult for your colleagues. Everyone can be cold and give up, making it difficult for them to communicate and work together or even get very heated.

There will be conflict over nothing, backstabbing or sabotaging, and endless office drama and rumors.

6. Office Conflict

Sometimes, it can be difficult to end a friendship with a college buddy and break up with a colleague. Being coworkers doesn't automatically mean you are immune to "breakups."

Another workplace drama comes when you must decide between two colleagues for a promotion or project. How can you pick without irritating people?

How to Disconnect from a Coworker or Friend

These are ways to avoid making fake friends at work.

1. Keep Your Boundaries

Keep a clear distinction between personal and professional ties. It's fine to be friendly with your employees. It's also a good idea to develop deeper relationships but keep the lines clear.

Remember that you and your coworkers are part of a professional organization. It's better to keep your distance if you still determine if the disclosure is necessary.

2. Keep your distance

Only spend a little time working with your coworkers to be popular or wealthy. It is possible to have a healthy relationship between friendship and work, but they should be manageable. You want work to be familiar and as comfortable as possible.

Stay away from the table with others when you go to lunch. You should only be involved in projects if something goes right. As much as possible, don't let your new friends know that you are employed at your workplace.

2. Use a filter

Some people have trouble controlling their speech and find it difficult to control their emotions. You don't have to tell your employees about your current relationship. However, you can relate to a funny story from years back. Although you could talk about your long-term goals and emphasize this relationship's temporary nature, it's unnecessary.

3. Being friendly and becoming friends

There is a huge difference between being cordial and being friends. Only 2% of employees consider their coworker's enemies. It is important to maintain positive, pleasant interactions with your coworkers. They are friends, but not your best friend.

4. Keep your Social Media Accounts Clear of Colleagues

This is a good guideline, but it's something only some follow. Don't add employees as Facebook friends.

Instead, create Instagram followers or share your Tiktok page with them.

Social media makes filtering hard. Using WhatsApp, group chats, and phone calls to communicate with employees is best.

5. Avoid Drama and Gossip

It is important to avoid Drama and not react to it. This will help you keep your life calm. For example, don't slander coworkers behind closed doors. This will only encourage more gossip and office turmoil. There is nothing wrong with maintaining good relations with your coworkers.

Sometimes a friend is enough to save you and your relationships at work. A friend who is a good friend will not get distracted by workplace drama and will refrain from spreading rumors.

A good friend will be able to spot any signs of trouble and provide private advice to assist you in making the right decisions. Keep in mind that everyone has a boss. Therefore, your coworkers don't have to be responsible for your professional development or happiness.

6. Never Date Your Coworkers

You shouldn't date a coworker, no matter how amazing they might seem. It is not worth the risk, trust me. Although you may feel the joy of falling in love with someone, it's not worth losing out on anything. Sometimes the people you aren't meant to be with, or the forbidden fruits seem more attractive than they are.

You might have few friends outside of work, but it is hard to ignore your coworkers. You should never forget the expression, "work colleagues don't count as your friends." Respect your professional boundaries to avoid stressing out and making career mistakes.

CHAPTER 4

Emotional Boundaries At Workplace

This is the difference between personal behavior and your business.

Emotional boundaries limit what somebody expects you to do at work based on an appropriate personal, professional, and legal boundary. When you have a huge shift in one of those arenas, it can lead to confusion or conflict in your work environment.

The following are examples of boundaries:

Wearing a suit to work instead of jeans while delivering pizzas.

Making phone calls outside of work hours.

Bringing your family dog to work with you every day.

Emotional boundaries happen when somebody has an expectation that doesn't mesh with what is possible for the other person's lifestyle or company policy.

The boundaries could be anything from expecting you to have a big family to work, being nice to the company's biggest customer, or dressing up for work.

Complaining about another employee is one of the most common ways to violate emotional boundaries. It's common for people to feel uncomfortable when they are around somebody else who is complaining non-stop while being unproductive at work.

Another thing that leads to emotional boundaries is smoking and drinking in the workplace. Some employees may take it as a personal attack if another person doesn't like the taste of their smoke or alcohol. Behaviors like these don't fit into an office setting and can lead to negative feelings towards your co-worker or manager.

Another way that emotional boundaries are broken is when you leave your personal problems to spill over into your work life. One example is stress at home or in a relationship spilling over into the workplace and causing conflict.

This can lead to distraction, increased sick time, and possibly even employees not working as hard as they could otherwise be.

Emotional boundaries can also arise when you break the company's unwritten rules. One example is showing up late or leaving early without anybody noticing; this can create tensions in the workplace because it might make other people think that they could do the same thing and get away with it too.

Emotional boundaries can sometimes also result from being too friendly with your co-workers.

Somebody can be friends with everybody, and it can make everybody uncomfortable; this is when the friendship develops into something more than that, like a romantic relationship.

Personal boundaries are what define your personal and business life.

It's important to know how much you need to control your personal life and work. Sometimes people try to work at home because they don't like the hours at work or have flexibility in their work schedule from home.

This can easily streamline into an obsession, making them more of a workaholic. An example of this is an employee who works from home and is constantly on the clock.

Email and text messaging are also exampling of personal boundaries. Text messages and emails can be very distracting regarding your work life because you don't know how long it will take to respond, when you get a response, if you will get one at all, if the person is mad at you for not responding promptly, etc.

Text messages can also be perceived as flirtatious; this could lead to conflict between people who are married or have significant others outside of work. Also, this can lead to bullying if you're a female in a male-dominated workplace.

Another example of someone violating personal boundaries is coming in late to work.

If you are hired into a job and expect to start at 7 a.m. doing the same tasks as your teammates, you can't just come in whenever you feel like it and do that same job at home or wherever else you choose to do it.

There is a certain amount of respect for your job position that needs to be done, especially by those who are hired into the position.

Another way that personal boundaries are violated is when you have too much time off or have too much flexibility in your schedule.

If you have too much time off, then people could perceive it as a means to try and avoid work.

This can lead to problems because you spend more time with your friends and family; this will also cause other employees to get jealous of what you're doing instead of working on their jobs.

If your hours need to be structured more so that your job doesn't take up all of your time, you could be doing things unrelated to the job. This can distract you from work, causing you to slack off on work because there is more free time.

Another example of personal boundaries being violated is being friends with your co-workers in an unhealthy way.

Your personal and professional lives can become intertwined in a very negative way; this can lead to problems because you could be spending too much time at work or not enough time with the other people involved in the relationship.

It can also lead to conflict with your work environment if one of you has a bad day and takes it out on your partner at work or vice versa. This can also create tension between co-workers and cause them not to want to be around that person anymore.

Another form of violating personal boundaries is if you decide to start a relationship with your co-worker.

If you have an opposite-sex friend, then it can lead to your co-workers feeling uncomfortable about it. This can cause them to be jealous because they feel like someone is taking their job away from them.

It can cause problems with colleagues and give the perception that you are trying to get something from the person by being friends with them. It also creates trust issues between the two of you, which could cause problems later on down the road when working in the same field again.

Emotional boundaries are the limits we set for ourselves and others around emotional expression, communication, and engagement.

In the workplace, emotional boundaries are critical for maintaining healthy and productive relationships, preventing burnout, and promoting personal well-being. This article will explore the importance of emotional boundaries at work, the challenges in setting and enforcing them, and strategies for establishing and maintaining healthy emotional boundaries.

Why Are Emotional Boundaries at Work Important?

Emotional boundaries at work are essential for several reasons:

Promoting Personal Well-Being: Emotional boundaries help us prioritize mental and emotional health by preventing emotional burnout and stress.

Establishing Professionalism: Emotional boundaries establish clear guidelines for appropriate workplace behavior and communication, promoting a professional work environment.

Encouraging Respectful Relationships: Emotional boundaries encourage respectful and supportive workplace relationships by promoting clear communication, empathy, and mutual respect.

Preventing Workplace Conflict: By setting clear emotional boundaries, we can avoid misunderstandings and conflicts in the workplace and maintain positive working relationships.

Challenges in Setting and Enforcing Emotional Boundaries at Work

While emotional boundaries are essential for maintaining a healthy workplace, setting and enforcing them can be challenging. Some common challenges in setting and enforcing emotional boundaries at work include:

Fear of Repercussions: Employees may fear that setting emotional boundaries will result in negative repercussions such as reduced job security, negative evaluations, or social exclusion.

Cultural or Organizational Norms: Workplace cultures or organizational norms may prioritize intense emotional engagement or suppression, creating conflict with emotional boundary-setting.

Difficulty in Communicating Needs: Some individuals may struggle with communicating their emotional needs or have a history of trauma that makes emotional expression difficult or uncomfortable.

Lack of Clarity: Emotional boundaries can be difficult to establish and enforce when there is a lack of clarity around job expectations, responsibilities, and communication channels.

Strategies for Establishing and Maintaining Healthy Emotional Boundaries at Work

Despite these challenges, several strategies exist for establishing and maintaining healthy emotional boundaries at work. Some of these include:

Self-Awareness: The first step in establishing healthy emotional boundaries is to become aware of one's emotional needs, limitations, and triggers. This involves reflecting on one's emotional responses to workplace situations and identifying areas where boundaries are needed.

Clear Communication: Effective communication is essential for setting and maintaining emotional workplace boundaries. This involves communicating needs and expectations clearly and respectfully, negotiating flexible work arrangements, and setting clear response times.

Developing Emotional Regulation Skills: Emotional regulation skills, such as mindfulness, deep breathing, and cognitive reframing, can help individuals manage their emotional responses in the workplace and prevent burnout.

Learning to Say "No": Learning to say "no" to unreasonable or emotionally demanding requests is an essential part of emotional boundary-setting. This requires developing assertiveness skills, practicing saying "no" to small requests, and developing a plan for addressing difficult or uncomfortable situations.

Recognizing and Addressing Emotional Boundary Violations: Emotional boundary violations can take many forms, including emotional manipulation, gaslighting, or excessive emotional demands on one's time and energy.

It is important to understand what constitutes an emotional boundary violation clearly and have strategies to address these situations.

Seeking Support: Setting and maintaining emotional boundaries can be challenging, and it is important to seek support and guidance from trusted colleagues or professionals when necessary.

Emotional boundaries at work are critical for maintaining healthy and productive workplace relationships, promoting personal well-being, and preventing burnout. By becoming more self-aware, communicating effectively, developing emotional regulation skills, and learning to say "no," individuals can establish and maintain healthy emotional boundaries at work.

CHAPTER 5

Physical Boundaries At Work

People forced to work within a shared workspace will be more creative because they will be mandated to use their collective skills. On the other hand, people desiring greater freedom were less likely to be satisfied with working in a group.

This might seem like a no-brainer: why wouldn't everyone want independence and space? But what happens when everyone is expected to work together? Will the same benefits result from being given free?

The answer is complex and lies in understanding how we relate ourselves psychologically and emotionally to physical boundaries.

If people can choose their working space, this chapter means they will be more creative and productive.

This is because the freedom provided by choice means that people can work independently without being forced to work alongside others with conflicting ideas.

People who need privacy to be creative will not feel inhibited without colleagues - they will not be blocked or stifled by other people's ideas.

The study found that people who need private space to be creative and productive and who need to avoid social interaction will enhance their productivity. After all, they will not be forced to share an office.

If people are given a space of their own, what happens if they choose not to use it? This can happen if a person feels they want more social interaction or a specific environment in which to work.

What happens if people choose not to give themselves space? This varies between individuals depending on how much independence they require.

If people are forced to occupy the same workspace, on the other hand, they will be more likely to collaborate. In a shared space, people are likelier to have an idea that another team member can support.

This collaborative feeling can also work in reverse: if a person feels they want to work together with their colleagues, they might be more motivated to help each other out.

They can lend each other support, like a "safety net." However, this reciprocal relationship sits on the assumption that everyone is willing to give and take equally - which might not always be the case

This shows us how complex it will be to create an environment that allows everyone, including effective collaboration. But could a space be designed to balance these two viewpoints?

The answer is yes. Physical boundaries can be managed to create the best environment for whatever needs and requirements are required.

This means that the physical space given is not absolute; rather, it will grow and develop, depending on what the workplace or individual workers are fulfilling needs.

Within this more flexible environment, people's first thoughts are to create one big open room and let everyone get on with their own thing without having any contact with each other. But this is only sometimes appropriate or possible, especially if different rules depending on which team a person works in.

A one size fits all solution is not always the best because it doesn't consider people's different needs and requirements. Instead, buildings designed to suit everyone's needs will be more likely to succeed in the long run.

The environment should be designed to encourage independent working for those who want autonomy and freedom, but also collaborative spaces for those who need support from others.

These different areas can encourage people to move around during the day - they will be able to socialize (if they want) or find a quiet place if they need space from other workers.

Physical boundaries at work refer to the limits we set for ourselves and others around physical touch, personal space, and access to our personal belongings.

Setting physical boundaries in the workplace is essential for maintaining a professional and respectful work environment, promoting personal safety and well-being, and preventing physical harassment or assault.

This chapter will explore the importance of physical boundaries at work, the challenges in setting and enforcing them, and strategies for establishing and maintaining healthy physical boundaries.

Why Are Physical Boundaries at Work Important?

Physical boundaries at work are essential for several reasons:

Maintaining Professionalism: Physical boundaries establish appropriate workplace behavior and communication guidelines, promoting a professional work environment.

Promoting Personal Safety: Physical boundaries help prevent physical harassment or assault, promoting personal safety and well-being.

Encouraging Respectful Relationships: Physical boundaries encourage respectful and supportive workplace relationships by promoting clear communication, empathy, and mutual respect.

Preventing Workplace Conflict: By setting clear physical boundaries, we can avoid misunderstandings and conflicts in the workplace and maintain positive working relationships.

Challenges in Setting and Enforcing Physical Boundaries at Work

While physical boundaries are essential for maintaining a healthy workplace, setting and enforcing them can be challenging. Some common challenges in setting and enforcing physical boundaries at work include:

Fear of Repercussions: Employees may fear that setting physical boundaries will result in negative repercussions such as reduced job security, negative evaluations, or social exclusion.

Cultural or Organizational Norms: Workplace cultures or organizational norms may prioritize physical touch or create pressure to share personal belongings, creating conflict with physical boundary-setting.

Difficulty in Communicating Needs: Some individuals may struggle with communicating their physical needs or have a history of trauma that makes physical touch uncomfortable or triggering.

Lack of Clarity: Physical boundaries can be difficult to establish and enforce without clarity around job expectations, responsibilities, and communication channels.

Strategies for Establishing and Maintaining Healthy Physical Boundaries at Work

Despite these challenges, several strategies exist for establishing and maintaining healthy physical boundaries at work. Some of these include:

Self-Awareness: The first step in establishing healthy physical boundaries is to become aware of one's physical needs, limitations, and triggers. This involves reflecting on one's physical responses to workplace situations and identifying areas where boundaries are needed.

Clear Communication: Effective communication is essential for setting and maintaining physical boundaries at work. This involves communicating needs and expectations clearly and respectfully, negotiating flexible work arrangements, and setting clear response times.

Developing Assertiveness Skills: Assertiveness skills, such as standing up for oneself and setting clear boundaries, can help individuals feel more comfortable asserting their physical boundaries in the workplace.

Practicing Saying "No": Learning to say "no" to unreasonable or physically demanding requests is essential to physical boundary-setting. This requires practicing saying "no" to small requests and developing a plan for addressing difficult or uncomfortable situations.

Recognizing and Addressing Physical Boundary Violations:

Physical boundary violations can take many forms, including unwanted physical touch, invasion of personal space, or theft of personal belongings.

It is important to clearly understand what constitutes a physical boundary violation and have strategies to address these situations.

Seeking Support: Setting and maintaining physical boundaries can be challenging, and it is important to seek support and guidance from trusted colleagues or professionals when necessary.

Tips and Tricks for Setting Physical Boundaries at Work

Here are some additional tips and tricks for setting physical boundaries at work:

Be clear and direct in your communication: Use clear language to communicate your physical boundaries, and be direct in your communication. For example, "I do not feel comfortable with physical touch

Set clear expectations: Set clear expectations for your physical boundaries with your coworkers, supervisor, or manager. This can involve setting expectations around physical touch, access to personal belongings, and communication channels.

Be proactive: Take a proactive approach to physical boundary-setting by communicating your needs and expectations early in the working relationship. This can help prevent misunderstandings or conflicts down the line.

Establish physical cues: Establish physical cues, such as hand gestures or body language, to indicate when your physical boundaries are being violated. This can help communicate your boundaries non-verbally and less aggressively.

Practice mindfulness: Being more aware of your physical needs and limits can help you become more mindful. This means paying attention to your body's feelings and thinking about your needs and limits.

Take breaks when you need to: Take breaks when you need to in order to refocus and recharge. This can help you avoid getting physically tired and allow you to set new physical limits.

Ask for help when you need it. When you need help, ask trusted coworkers, friends, or professionals. This can help you avoid getting physically tired and let you set new physical limits.

When you need help, ask for it. Ask trusted coworkers, friends, or professionals for help when needed. This can mean asking for help setting physical boundaries or helping people break physical boundaries.

Janice had just started a new job at a small company that was just getting started. She was excited about the job and its opportunities, but she quickly realized that her physical boundaries were being crossed.

Her coworkers often came up behind her and touched her back or shoulder without her permission, and sometimes her boss went through her things without asking. Janice felt uneasy and violated, but she was afraid to say anything because she didn't want to lose her job.

After a few weeks, Janice realized she needed to set clear physical boundaries at work. She began by reflecting on her physical needs and limitations and identifying areas where her boundaries were violated. She then conversed with her supervisor, explaining her physical boundaries and asking for respect. She also spoke with her coworkers, using clear and direct language to communicate her physical boundaries and expectations.

At first, Janice's coworkers and supervisor were taken aback by her assertiveness. However, they quickly realized the importance of respecting Janice's physical boundaries and adjusted their behavior accordingly.

Janice felt more comfortable and respected in her workplace and could focus on her job without the distractions and discomfort of physical boundary violations.

Setting physical boundaries at work is essential for maintaining a professional and respectful work environment, promoting personal safety and well-being, and preventing physical harassment or assault. While setting and enforcing physical boundaries can be challenging, there are several strategies and tips for establishing and maintaining healthy physical boundaries at work.

By becoming more self-aware, practicing clear communication, and seeking support, individuals can set and maintain healthy physical boundaries in the workplace.

CHAPTER 6

How To Set Time Boundaries At Workplace

Time boundaries are a great way to improve productivity, reduce distractions and encourage focus. When faced with a time-sensitive project or task, set aside a specific block of time for it and keep yourself from doing anything else.

This helps you get a full and deep focus on the task at hand. Don't let yourself be distracted halfway through your workday, or you'll finish only a portion.

Time boundaries are not set in stone – they're just a good rule of thumb that you can use to help you stay productive. If an important email comes in or someone else needs to speak with you, don't ignore that! Just finish what you're doing and reply to the email or attend to whoever needs something from you.

If you need help focusing on a task for a long time, it might be because you have too much time. Your mind starts to wander, and before you know it, you're distracted and need to accomplish what you set out to do.

Try breaking down your tasks into smaller, more manageable chunks so that your mind doesn't have as far to wander when working on them.

For a healthy work/life balance and to prevent burnout, it is important to establish time boundaries at work. Time boundaries allow you to limit the time you devote to work-related tasks and limit your availability for meetings. This chapter will give you a detailed guide for setting time limits at work.

Identify your time priorities

Priorities are the first step in setting work time boundaries. This may involve identifying your most crucial tasks and responsibilities and setting goals and deadlines. By prioritizing your tasks and responsibilities, you can better manage time and allocate the right amount of time to each project or task.

Define your work hours.

It is crucial to establish work boundaries. This means establishing your work hours and communicating with others. To avoid conflicts or misunderstandings, it is crucial to communicate clearly your work hours to coworkers and supervisors.

Set Limits on Communication

Setting limits on communication is another important component of setting time boundary at work. This involves defining your preferred communication methods and setting limits on your availability for communication outside of your work hours.

Establishing a clear communication policy with your coworkers and supervisors can be helpful to ensure that everyone is on the same page.

Take Breaks

For productivity to be maintained and burnout prevention, it is essential that you take breaks throughout your day. It can be as simple as taking short breaks to recharge and refocus throughout the day. Or it could mean taking longer breaks for lunch or other self-care activities; your supervisors and coworkers should be informed about your schedule, so they are well-informed.

Avoid Over-Committing

You must be as productive as possible during your workday. It is important to prioritize and avoid over-committing.

Over-commitment can lead to burnout. It is essential to establish clear boundaries and prioritize your tasks. This will help you identify the tasks that must be completed to continue with your work responsibilities.

It is helpful to divide tasks and projects you want to accomplish during work hours. This helps you focus on the task and keeps distractions at bay.

Establish time boundaries for other tasks.

Some tasks and projects might not be possible during your regular work hours. You can set time limits for these tasks to ensure you have enough time to complete them on time.

Time Boundaries During Special Occasions

Time boundaries can get complicated when dealing with special occasions, such as company events and celebrations.

Use Time Management Tools

Using time management tools can help set time boundaries at work. This can involve using a calendar or scheduling app to manage your tasks and deadlines and time-tracking software to monitor your time on work-related tasks.

These tools help you stay organized and dedicate the appropriate amount of time to each task or project.

Delegate Tasks

Delegating tasks is another important component of setting time boundary at work. This involves identifying tasks that can be delegated to other team members and seeking support from coworkers and supervisors when necessary.

Delegating tasks can help you manage your workload more effectively and ensure you dedicate the appropriate amount of time to each task or project.

Practice Saying "No"

Practicing saying "no" is essential to set time boundaries at work. This involves setting boundaries on your availability for additional tasks or projects and declining invitations to meetings or events that do not align with your priorities. It can be helpful to communicate your reasons for saying "no" clearly to your coworkers and supervisors to avoid misunderstandings or conflicts.

Use Time Boundaries to Foster Collaboration

Time boundaries can also be used to foster collaboration at work. This can involve setting time boundaries for meetings, communicating your availability, and sticking to these boundaries when working with your coworkers. It is essential to clearly communicate your time boundaries to avoid confusion or misunderstandings with your coworkers.

Set clear goals on how you want the people in your life to treat you, and then make sure that they adhere explicitly and unequivocally to these rules if they don't, discuss it (or dump them).

Setting time boundaries at work is essential for achieving a healthy work-life balance and preventing burnout. It involves identifying your time priorities, defining your work hours, setting limits on communication, taking breaks, using time management tools, delegating tasks, and practicing saying "no.

" These strategies and tips can establish effective time boundaries and create a healthy and productive work environment.

CHAPTER 7

Mental Boundaries At Work

Mental Boundaries: Your mental boundaries refer to your thoughts, values, and opinions on matters in the workplace. For example, you might have your opinion on how things should operate at work and value your morning meetings — and you won't allow someone else's ideas of how things should go to influence your own.

A mental boundary is one you consciously choose to put up to prevent your feelings from being controlled or dictated by someone else. Simply, it's a boundary that won't let others tell you what to do. It's an important but often troubling concept for some people because it can be misused.

This could be for selfish reasons, such as when you want someone to promote you — and then fire someone else. Or it could be for more seemingly noble reasons, like when you want the boss in another department to listen to your idea before dismissing it outright.

Mental boundaries can seem confusing, yet there are rules in place that can help with their understanding and management. For example, you might have a boundary between your personal and professional lives.

Perhaps you're trying to impress your boss by reading up on what they are concerned with — or trying to learn all the possible ways that you can impress him by being with him often.

In each case, you must consider the potential impact on your job performance and how others might feel about it.

As for how people handle and manage boundaries within their personal lives, there are many different options. Some people may avoid certain topics or behaviors entirely.

Others may arrange a mutually comfortable compromise between their boundaries and those of others. Perhaps you have friends who are good about respecting your personal boundaries — but don't always do the same for you in your professional life.

Mental boundaries can be either invisible or very obvious — depending on how the people around them handle them. You may want someone to respect your mental boundaries at home and at work or vice versa — but in one case or another, a problem can arise.

Mental boundaries are defined by two broad categories: those that are outer — those that relate to who, where, and when we work — and those that are inner — those relating to how we work. The following sections cover both types in more detail.

Outer boundaries:

Outer boundaries are those that are important to other people and that affect how they perceive our work.

They include rules such as showing up on time, following the dress code, and respecting the privacy of others. For example, you might have a boundary that requires you to always follow the rules at work. Or you could have a boundary of not gossiping about other employees or your superiors.

...what is it:

A mental boundary is a rule we set to stop others from telling us what to do or influencing us in any way, shape, or form. It's important to remember that it is a rule, not an absolute — and can be changed.

...why do you need it:

We all have our own boundaries, and we need them to ensure that we can work in an environment where our wants, needs, and what we want to achieve are considered.

For example, you may have your morning meeting routine, meaning you wake up early and don't bother anyone else by entering the office before they arrive. You may also have a boundary about having personal conversations while at work. It's important to avoid getting caught up in discussing things other than working with others.

You might have heard of the fourth wall, that pesky thing in the theater. Mental boundaries at work are like the fourth wall but for work. They refer to the invisible line between your mind and your job.

There's a whole lot of research out there about how to be more productive at work; most of it involves getting rid of distractions and surrounding yourself with only what you need for the task at hand: as soon as you cross into thinking about anything else, your productivity is basically done for.

But what if the thing you're meant to be focusing on is precisely what you don't want to think about? Mental boundaries at work are your fourth wall: they're the barrier that prevents you from confronting a distasteful boss, an unfair workload, or a big project that you would rather be left for another time.

Mental boundaries are when you're working and not working simultaneously because you're thinking about everything but work.

And that's exactly what makes them so useful. Mental boundaries allow us to manage our stress at work and keep on working.

They're how we build up the strength to confront things we otherwise wouldn't be able to handle, like talking back to a partner who says something obnoxious in front of the kids or saying no to an unreasonable client.

For mental boundaries to be effective, you need two things:

First, you have a reason for having the boundary that goes beyond the inconvenience of having it there.

Secondly, you have to know your breaking point.

That unpleasant discomfort causes you to start shutting down and wishing it would all just go away — even if "it" means your job. Knowing your breaking point will allow you to maximize the use of your personal boundaries because you'll know when it's time to start working on them.

Mental boundaries help us deal with our jobs in a way that makes us stronger and more able to get through the tough parts. Being able to deal with changes at work can happen when we can change our minds and know when we need to change.

Our mental boundaries enhance our ability to adapt and make ourselves stronger. With mental boundaries, we can transform whatever comes our way into something that strengthens us and makes us better able to handle the next time.

Creating a healthy and positive work environment.

Understand the Importance of Mental Boundaries

The first step in setting mental boundaries at work is understanding their importance. Setting mental boundaries can help you maintain your well-being, reduce stress and burnout, and enhance productivity and job satisfaction. It is important to recognize that setting mental boundaries is not a sign of weakness or unprofessionalism but rather a vital component of maintaining your mental health and well-being.

Identify Your Triggers and Limitations

Identifying your triggers and limitations is critical to setting mental boundaries at work. This involves recognizing the situations or interactions that drain your mental and emotional energy and your limitations in terms of workload and responsibilities.

By identifying your triggers and limitations, you can better manage your mental and emotional energy and dedicate the appropriate amount of time and attention to each task or interaction.

Communicate Your Boundaries Clearly

Communicating your mental boundaries clearly to your coworkers and supervisors is essential for ensuring your needs are respected, and your well-being is prioritized.

This involves setting clear expectations and boundaries for your workload, communication, and interactions. Communicating your boundaries respectfully and assertively can be helpful, emphasizing the importance of maintaining your well-being and productivity.

Practice Self-Care

Practicing self-care is a vital component of setting mental boundaries at work. This involves prioritizing activities and behaviors that support your mental and emotional well-being, such as exercise, mindfulness practices, and hobbies.

It is important to carve out time in your schedule for self-care activities and to communicate your needs to your coworkers and supervisors.

Set Realistic Goals and Expectations

Setting realistic goals and expectations is another important component of setting mental boundaries at work. This involves prioritizing your workload and setting achievable goals and deadlines.

It is important to clearly communicate your goals and expectations to your coworkers and supervisors and seek support when necessary.

Practice Mindfulness and Self-Awareness

Practicing mindfulness and self-awareness is essential for setting and maintaining mental boundaries at work. This involves tuning into your mental and emotional state, recognizing your triggers and limitations, and responding to challenging situations calmly and centered manner. Practicing mindfulness techniques, such as meditation or deep breathing, can be helpful throughout the day in maintaining focus and mental clarity.

Seek Support When Necessary

Seeking support when necessary is crucial to setting and maintaining mental boundaries at work. This involves reaching out to coworkers, supervisors, or mental health professionals when you feel overwhelmed or struggle with your workload or responsibilities. It is important to prioritize your well-being and to seek support when necessary to maintain your mental and emotional health.

Setting mental boundaries at work are essential for maintaining your well-being and productivity. It involves understanding the importance of mental boundaries, identifying your triggers and limitations, communicating your boundaries, practicing self-care, setting realistic goals and expectations, practicing mindfulness and self-awareness, and seeking support when necessary.

Following these strategies and tips can establish effective mental boundaries and create a healthy and positive work environment.

CHAPTER 8

Priority And Workload Boundaries

To perform at your best, you must protect your workload with firm, healthy boundaries. Every day or week, many team members will ask you for help. This is great—they think you're skilled and value your contributions! But if you accommodate every request, you'll be frazzled and unproductive.

Remember, you only get so many hours in a week. It's simply not possible to take on everything.

The first step in protecting your workload is to define your sense of priority. Here are some questions to ponder:

• Am I really the best person to tackle this work request? If not, could I recommend someone who is a better fit?

• Am I willing and able to do this work within the time frame needed? If not, can we negotiate a different timeline?

The second step is establishing workload boundaries, limiting what you will and will not do. For each project or task, you're currently working on, decide how long you will devote to it and then specify that commitment.

For example, if it's more than two weeks and up to 20 hours of work, write an estimate of that work on your calendar. Also, this task is limited to the first week of each month.

You may want to add other tasks or projects you don't want to do within your capacity. There's nothing wrong with making space for more weighty activities occasionally, but it's best not to feel like you have too much on your plate all the time.

The goal is to maintain momentum, focus on priorities, and not feel like too many balls are in the air. You're far more likely to accomplish more by sticking to your tasks rather than juggling too many things at a time.

Workload boundaries also provide a way for you to let go of projects that aren't working out or aren't as important as you might have thought from the start.

• Do I have enough information to estimate this work request?

• What are my limits on scope, schedule, and commitment?

• How do I communicate these limits to others?

This exercise is not about denying what you want or pretending you are not obligated to help a co-worker. It's about establishing healthy priorities and boundaries to respond positively to decisive support requests.

Be proactive: define your priorities, set your boundaries, and stick with them. If you're asked to drop everything to help someone, ask how soon they need a response and whether or not you can provide the support. If they say, they don't really need it right now, be honest and say you can't do it.

One other thing: remember that work is inherently good and good. Work is a way we create value for others by providing them with what they need to flourish.

So when someone asks for your time, ask yourself if it will truly bring them value or if this request has more to do with their needs than yours.

• Is this a necessary request?

• Am I willing and able to provide all the value requested within my capacity?

• Is what's being asked of me aligned with my priorities, or am I being asked to do more urgent things than important?

Priority and workload boundaries are essential tools in time management. They help individuals to prioritize tasks and allocate time efficiently to meet deadlines.

In today's fast-paced world, it is easy to become overwhelmed by the sheer volume of work that needs to be done. However, by setting priorities and workload boundaries, individuals can manage their time effectively and achieve their goals without feeling stressed or overworked.

What are Priority and Workload Boundaries?

Priority boundaries refer to setting priorities for different tasks based on their importance and urgency.

Workload boundaries, however, refer to the amount of work that can be handled within a given timeframe. Setting workload boundaries is crucial for preventing burnout and ensuring tasks are completed within the specified time.

The Importance of Setting Priority and Workload Boundaries

The benefits of setting priority and workload boundaries are numerous:

It allows individuals to focus on tasks that are most important and urgent. This ensures that critical tasks are completed within the given timeframe and there is no last-minute rush.

Setting priority and workload boundaries can help individuals to avoid burnout. Individuals can avoid becoming overwhelmed and stressed by limiting the amount of work that can be handled within a given timeframe.

Setting priority and workload boundaries can help individuals to achieve a healthy work-life balance.

It allows individuals to allocate time to other important aspects of their lives, such as family, friends, and hobbies.

How to Set Priority and Workload Boundaries

Setting priority and workload boundaries is challenging, but it can be done effectively with some guidance. Here are some steps to follow when setting priority and workload boundaries:

Identify your goals and objectives.

Before setting priority and workload boundaries, it is essential to identify your goals and objectives. This will help you determine the most important and urgent tasks. Setting goals and objectives allow you to prioritize tasks aligned with your goals and objectives.

List your tasks

Once you have identified your goals and objectives, the next step is to list all the tasks that must be completed. This includes both professional and personal tasks. By listing all the tasks, you can clearly understand what needs to be done.

Determine the importance and urgency of each task.

After listing all the tasks, the next step is to determine the importance and urgency of each task. This involves asking yourself questions such as, "Is this task essential to achieving my goals and objectives?" and "Is this task time-sensitive?" By determining the importance and urgency of each task, you can prioritize the most important and urgent tasks.

Allocate time for each task.

Once you have prioritized your tasks, the next step is to allocate time for each task. This involves setting workload boundaries. For instance, you can allocate specific hours for work-related tasks and the remaining time for personal tasks.

Review your progress regularly.

It is essential to review your progress regularly to determine whether you are on track. This involves monitoring the tasks that have been completed and those that are yet to be completed. Reviewing your progress regularly allows you to plan and ensure you meet your goals and objectives.

In conclusion, setting priority and workload boundaries is essential for managing time effectively. It helps individuals to prioritize tasks and allocate time efficiently to meet deadlines. By setting workload boundaries, individuals can prevent burnout and ensure that tasks are completed within the given timeframe.

It also helps to achieve a healthy work-life balance and focus on other important aspects of life. It is essential to review progress regularly and adjust meet goals and objectives. By following the steps outlined in this article, individuals can set priority and workload boundaries effectively and manage their time efficiently.

CHAPTER 9

Resolving Workplace Conflict

Conflict is costly and can have a wide-ranging impact on the workplace. As three researchers have demonstrated, conflict is a common problem in the workplace.

It accounts for between 20 and 40 percent of all management time. This causes decreased productivity, stress among employees, and high turnover rates. It can also lead to absenteeism, low performance, and violence, resulting in death.

Many employees don't realize the reasons for conflict or its consequences in their work environment. This paper aims to describe the phenomenon and suggest ways to reduce conflict at work.

This paper seeks to provide readers with an understanding of how "conflict" works in their daily lives. Modern times are marked by high levels, unpredictable stress levels, increasing tempo-sparing tasks, unreasonable expectations, and a lack of ability to meet them. These emotions and behavior can lead to frustration, anger, resentfulness, anxiety, and even anger.

An investigation by the University of Wisconsin found that 55% of managers spend their time dealing with anger. This is true at all levels of management, from Supervisors to Managers.

Employee productivity drops, and the workplace becomes more stressful. Employees have complained about losing time due to having to deal at work with anger.

There are many reasons for conflict in the workplace. Feeling taken advantage of is the main cause. This can happen when a boss demands perfection from employees but does nothing to compensate them for working late or on weekends. Employees feeling, they aren't valued is another cause of conflict.

This can happen when employees feel underpaid, or their employer does not allow them to speak up at work. Sometimes, jealousy, envy, or rivalry can lead to co-worker conflict.

A person who feels threatened or jealous over another person's success may try to cause conflict by making them look better.

Others include employees having unrealistic job expectations and being misunderstood in the workplace. Values and company goal differences can also lead to conflict.

The company may need more goals or adequately communicate its values and goals to employees. However, an employee might have different goals and values than the company.

There are four things managers can do to reduce workplace conflicts. Managers can begin by examining their communication skills. This applies to both how they communicate and how employees communicate with one another. This includes using I statements as an alternative to your language. Communicating with your employees in this manner can reduce conflict.

Managers need to develop their listening skills. Active listening refers to actively listening. This involves trying to understand what the other person says and then communicating to that person that you understand their words.

A healthy boundary is another way to reduce workplace conflict. You will have conflict, squabbles, power struggles, and other circumstances that create messy situations.

You can still be professional and compassionate toward your employees without being a friend. This is especially important if there's a power differential between two individuals in an employment situation.

A skill called emotional intelligence is the third factor that can reduce conflict. It has many aspects and facets, but it means that people can learn to be more efficient by combining intelligence with emotions at work.

The busy workplace can make seeing and treating employees as individuals with real lives difficult. People with high emotional intelligence can do this professionally while maintaining appropriate boundaries. Another aspect of EQ is being able to recognize and be sensitive to employees' feelings about you as a leader. EQ is also about teaching managers how they present themselves to others. Do you come across as friendly or passive? Do you seem flirty or intimidating? Are you a confident or thoughtful person?

If you want to start your own small business, you must have good EQ skills. Because of the daily conflict in their lives, many self-employed people don't achieve their dreams. People with high EQs can solve problems and make better decisions.

A fourth aspect of reducing workplace conflict involves setting up behavioral consequences that can be used for truly uncooperative employees who refuse change. Some employees won't change, despite all the suggestions.

The manager must explain a consequence. A consequence is an action that warns the employee about the possible consequences of their continued bad behavior. You will need the skills outlined above to communicate this effectively in a non-threatening manner.

Is there ever a place to be angry in the workplace? Yes. If people can say, "Wait! People can say, I'm not happy about this. They turn anger into a positive activity. Anger can then be considered a motivator. Sometimes we can work with the company if we recognize when we are upset and turn that into a positive action.

Anger can be a useful emotion, but there are rules. To be constructive and positive in the workplace, we must remember anger is a survival emotion. Fear breeds fear. If you identify your fear, you can say: "Well, if my feelings of being valued or heard don't make me feel respected, then this is an angry business." And this will take me somewhere I won't feel the same way again.

Anger can be a powerful motivator for people and employees in emotional crises.

Employees should learn to speak out and be able and healthy to communicate their needs and desires.

Employees can alter their attitude to work while still enduring the difficult aspects. Changing our outlook and vision about why we were here is possible. This will help reduce conflict.

How we see the situation will determine our satisfaction and fulfillment at work.

It is easier to see the big picture without getting distracted by the details. When we have these big images and goals in mind, we will likely avoid getting bogged down by small problems.

"The only man who never makes any mistakes is he who never does anything." this means that as long we are actively learning and growing, we cannot limit what we can do. There will be mistakes along the way. However, how we learn from them determines our success at work and home.

Made in United States
Troutdale, OR
05/13/2024

19844243R00049